THE LATER YEARS OF BRITISH RAIL 1980–1995

Volume Three – West Midlands, Wales and South-West England

Patrick Bennett

First published 2018

Amberley Publishing
The Hill, Stroud
Gloucestershire, GL5 4EP

www.amberley-books.com

Copyright © Patrick Bennett, 2018

The right of Patrick Bennett to be identified as
the Author of this work has been asserted in
accordance with the Copyrights, Designs and
Patents Act 1988.

ISBN 978 1 4456 7520 6 (print)
ISBN 978 1 4456 7521 3 (ebook)

British Library Cataloguing in Publication Data.
A catalogue record for this book is available from
the British Library.

Origination by Amberley Publishing.

Contents

Introduction

The period 1980 to 1995 would see greater changes to Britain's railways than in any other time in their 150-year history. By 1980 the days of steam had gone but in other respects the railway had little changed. Long-distance trains still consisted for the most part of locomotives hauling carriages, while local services were in the hands of first generation diesel multiple units (DMUs), introduced in the mid-1950s. Freight traffic was still buoyant, although much of it was still being carried in the short-wheelbase wagons of the steam age. Marshalling yards were busy and there were many miles of freight sidings and branches. A large part of the network was still controlled by traditional signalling. One major change that had taken place was the disappearance of the regional identities, to be replaced by the universal corporate blue.

For the areas covered by this book there had been two significant changes. By 1966 the electrification of the routes from London to Liverpool and Manchester had been completed, leading to the introduction of new locomotives and rolling stock and the rebuilding of a number of stations. In the South West the introduction of the high speed train had brought about considerable improvements. Elsewhere things were much as before, but all that was about to change. In the early 1980s sectorisation arrived, accompanied by new liveries and 'branding'. At about the same time a new generation of multiple units started to be introduced, replacing many loco-hauled services. Resignalling proceeded apace while freight traffic declined. Finally, in the mid-1990s came privatisation, the exploding of the railway into a thousand fragments.

When compiling this book, twenty-three years after the last photograph was taken, what struck me very forcibly is that in this latter period the railway has changed to an even greater extent than in the preceding fifteen years. The passenger railway is now almost entirely in the hands of multiple units of various kinds. Freight has declined catastrophically, not least because of the closing down of the British mining industry. Many freight-only lines have closed and whole swathes of freight infrastructure – sidings, terminals, marshalling yards – have been swept way. Traditional signalling is becoming an endangered species, with vast areas controlled by single centres. Electrification has proceeded apace, if not without problems, and there have been a number of stations reopened for passenger use. The result of all this change is that the vast majority of images in this book depict scenes that have gone forever. They are in that sense historic.

The photographs that appear in the following pages are very much a personal collection, reflecting my own interests and to some extent my own travels. During the course of the period this volume covers my methodology in taking photographs changed. In 1988 I realised that the railway was changing at an ever increasing rate, many of its features disappearing forever. So it was, that from that time onwards, I tended to concentrate my efforts on what was shortly to be lost forever; this included older type of locomotives and rolling stock, traditional signalling, and particularly freight flows, sidings and freight-only lines. This volume also contains the work of other photographers and the author and publisher would like to thank the following for permission to use copyright material in this book: Chris Gwilliam for the photographs taken at Maindee, Llanwern, Cardiff, Wool, Parson's Tunnel and Truro; Ben Brooksbank for the photographs taken at Tondu, Croes Newydd, and Holyhead; and Peter Groom for the photograph taken at Exmouth Junction.

Millay, France
January, 2018

The West Midlands

Crewe to Chester

Crewe came into being as a railway station in 1837 with the opening of the Grand Junction Railway between Birmingham and Warrington. At that time Crewe was a hamlet of just 184 people on the estate of Lord Crewe, after whom the station was named. The Manchester to Birmingham railway opened between Manchester and Crewe in 1842. On 23 May 1992, No. 47095 passes through the station southbound with a train of BOC tanks.

On the same date No. 31432 leaves in the opposite direction with the 13.03 to Holyhead.

South of Crewe is Mill Meece, where we see a rare matching of Regional Railways locomotive and carriages, forming a Birmingham–Holyhead service. The engine is No. 37429 *Eisteddfod Genedlaethol*.

The Chester & Crewe Railway was incorporated in 1837 and opened its 21-mile line in October 1840. Before that, in July, it had been absorbed by the GJR. On 12 September 1981 we see No. 40139 approaching Chester with a special train.

Seen at the same location, a Class 103 DMU arrives with the 14.00 Manchester Oxford Road to Chester. Only twenty of these two-car Park Royal sets were built and all had been withdrawn by 1983.

A Class 103 unit paired with a Class 108 heads past the massive Chester No. 2 signal box with the 16.17 from Crewe.

In the summer of 1983 GWR locomotive No. 6000 *King George V* stands by Chester No. 4 signal box, waiting to back on to its train. On the right can be seen the former steam depot. Chester No. 4, along with its 176-lever frame, was commissioned in 1904. It was abolished, along with all the other mechanical boxes at Chester, in 1984, signalling being taken over by the new Chester power box.

There were originally five stations between Crewe and Chester; all were closed by 1966. Called plain Beeston when it was opened, it became Beeston Castle in 1868, and Beeston Castle and Tarporley in 1873. Unit No. 150243 heads through the closed station with the 14.34 Chester to Crewe. Beeston signal box, which remains open, is seen in the background. The subsidiary signal is for the Down loop, which has since been removed. 23 May 1991.

Crewe to Shrewsbury

The Crewe & Shrewsbury Railway, part of the LNW, opened throughout as a single line in 1858. The line was doubled four years later. Whitchurch became an important junction following the opening of the Oswestry, Ellesmere & Whitchurch Railway in 1863/4, and the LNW line from Whitchurch to Tattenhall Junction, on the Crewe–Chester line, in 1872. The Oswestry line closed in 1965 and the Tattenhall line in 1963. Whitchurch, which at one time had a staff of more than 100, now has no staff at all. On 28 March 1989 No. 47457 pilots No. 37456 with the 11.20 Liverpool to Cardiff. The Up loop and the two sidings no longer exist.

A Class 108 DMU heads past Wem signal box with a service for Shrewsbury. Following the resignalling of the line in October 2013, Wem box was closed, together with all the other signal boxes on the line. It was subsequently demolished. The line is now controlled from Cardiff.

The Shrewsbury & Hereford Railway was opened throughout in 1853. It was worked by the West Midland Railway, which later became part of the GWR. In 1862 the LNW secured a joint interest in the line but joint working did not begin until 1875. From that time each company ran their own trains and tickets were not interchangeable. This is a classic BR Blue era scene as Nos 37210 and 37278 plus Mk 1 rolling stock pull away from Shrewsbury with the Euston to Aberystwyth Cambrian Coast Express in August 1985.

In the same month No. 33043 arrives at Shrewsbury with a Cardiff–Manchester Piccadilly service. In the background is Severn Bridge Junction signal box. Its 180-lever frame makes it the largest mechanical signal box in the world. There are currently no plans to replace it.

On the same day No. 45006, running light engine, has derailed on the crossover alongside Sutton Bridge Junction signal box.

The permanent way staff were able to re-rail the engine without resorting to a crane but this left the track out of gauge, necessitating further work. No. 33043 has returned from Manchester and finally gets under way with the much delayed service for Cardiff. In the background No. 45006 can be seen parked in the refuge siding.

Waiting for the road at Sutton Bridge Junction, we once more see the Cambrian Coast Express. The date is 11 May 1991 and this is the penultimate day of loco haulage for the CCE. In contrast to the earlier photograph, the locomotives are in sector liveries, with No. 37430 in InterCity livery and No. 37421 in Construction Sector livery. The rolling stock has changed too, these being Mk 2 vehicles. The differing signals reflect Shrewsbury's history as a joint LNW/GW station. Of the three signals on the right, the left-hand one is for the Mid-Wales line, the centre for the Hereford line and the small signal on the right for the Down goods loop. The loop has now been lifted.

A view at Sutton Bridge taken facing the other direction shows DMU No. 155321 with the 15.35 Cardiff–Manchester Piccadilly. To the right is the Mid-Wales line, while straight on leads to Hereford and Cardiff. This view has changed considerably. The Down goods loop and the Coleham Shelf sidings on the left have all been lifted, as has the track on the extreme right. 11 May 1991.

A number of railway lines converged at Shrewsbury. The Shropshire & Montgomeryshire Railway opened in 1911 and lost its passenger service in 1933. It had its own station in Shrewsbury at Shrewsbury Abbey. Taken over by the MOD in 1941 to service the Nesscliffe ammunition depot, it finally closed in 1960. The GWR's Severn Valley line closed in 1963, although of course a large section is now a preserved railway. For the Shrewsbury & Chester Railway, see the section on Wales.

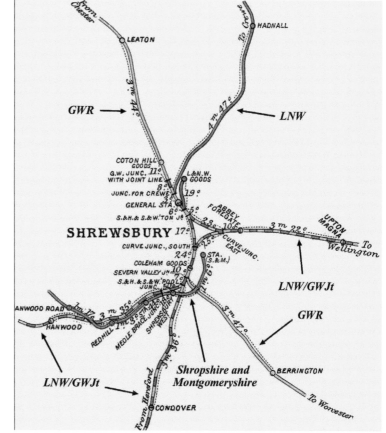

Shrewsbury to Wolverhampton

The line between Shrewsbury and Wellington was LNW/GW joint. The Shrewsbury & Birmingham Railway was authorised in 1846 and completed in 1849. The section between Wellington and Shrewsbury was built jointly by the GWR and the Shropshire Union Railways & Canal Company, who later leased their interest to the LNW. The station at Abbey Foregate closed to passengers as early as 1912 but stayed open for freight until 1963. A Class 150 heading for Shrewsbury passes under the magnificent gantry at Abbey Foregate in the summer of 1988. Sadly, the gantry was removed shortly after this photograph was taken.

Passing the site of the closed Upton Magna station is green-liveried No. 47500 *Great Western* with the Down Cambrian Coast Express on the penultimate day of loco haulage. 11 May 1991.

At Madeley Junction No. 150118 hurries past with the 13.25 Shrewsbury–Wolverhampton. The line to the left leads to Ironbridge power station. 24 May 1992.

Cosford station opened in 1937 to serve the nearby RAF camp. A pairing of a Class 158 and a Class 156 forms the 12.28 Aberystwyth–Birmingham as it approaches the station. Notice the upper quadrant semaphores on GWR dolls.

A photograph taken from the opposite direction shows a Wolverhampton–Chester service. The Up and Down goods loops still exist but the signal box has been abolished and the area is now controlled from Madeley Junction. 24 May 1992.

Shrewsbury to Hereford and Worcester

Of the original sixteen stations between Shrewsbury and Hereford, now only Church Stretton, Craven Arms, Ludlow and Leominster remain open. Dorrington is the location of one of the closed stations. On 31 August 1991 No. 47201 passes with a mixed freight. The signal box dates from 1872 and is due to be taken out of use in 2017. Notice the GWR lower quadrant signals, one of which has subsequently been replaced by a BR upper quadrant.

Church Stretton, and a southbound Class 108 DMU approaches the station. A redundant water column stands next to the signal.

At Hereford a Class 116 unit waits to leave with the 13.55 to Newport. The two through lines are the Up and Down relief. 15 July 1990.

The Worcester & Hereford Railway was opened progressively between 1859 and 1861. It was absorbed by the OWW, becoming part of the West Midland Railway, which in its turn became part of the GWR in 1863. At Great Malvern on 15 July 1990 a Class 156 DMU waits to leave with a service for Birmingham. Note the elaborate spandrels and decorated capitals supporting the platform canopy.

3 miles east of Great Malvern is the site of Newlands East signal box and level crossing. Tyseley's four–car Class 115 unit No. 402 heads towards Great Malvern with a service from Birmingham. The Down refuge siding seen on the right has been abolished. 15 July 1990.

'The Old Worse and Worse'

In 1845 the Oxford, Worcester & Wolverhampton Railway was authorised to build a railway from Oxford to Wolverhampton. It earned its sobriquet, among other reasons, for the length of time it took to complete the line, just 90 miles long. It finally opened throughout on 1 December 1853. The engineer for the line was I. K. Brunel, and Charlbury was a station built to his design. On a miserably damp August Bank Holiday in 1980 we see a very grubby No. 47237 arriving at the station with the 12.55 Paddington to Worcester Shrub Hill. The line at Charlbury was singled in 1971 and redoubled in 2011, at which time a second platform was added.

No. 155305 passes through Norton Junction with the 14.40 Oxford to Hereford. This is where the Midland Railway Birmingham–Gloucester line is met. There was once a station here, first called Norton Junction and then Norton Halt. After many years in the planning, work is due to start in 2017 on a new interchange station, with platforms on both lines. 17 March 1990.

At Worcester a Tyseley Class 116 DMU leaves with the 13.02 Birmingham New Street to Hereford. Notice the mechanical route indicator showing 'H'FORD' and also the fixed distants. In 1860 the OWW became part of the West Midlands Railway and then in 1863 part of the GWR. 17 March 1990.

On 25 May 1980 No. 50042 *Triumph* departs from Worcester with the 16.25 Hereford to Paddington. No. 50042 is one of the extraordinary number of eighteen of this class to survive into preservation and is currently stationed on the Bodmin & Wenford Railway.

This is a view taken from just above Rainbow Hill Tunnel. The lines to the right lead to Worcester Foregate Street, and those to the left to Shrub Hill. The signal box is Worcester Tunnel Junction.

A Class 116 unit arrives at Droitwich Spa with a service for Great Malvern. The lines to the left are the OWW route to Kidderminster and Stourbridge. Those to the right lead to the MR route to Birmingham via the Lickey Incline.

Stourbridge station opened in 1852. It became a junction in 1863 when the Stourbridge Railway opened its line to Cradley. In 1871 the Stourbridge Railway was incorporated into the GWR and it was they who opened the ¾-mile-long Stourbridge Town branch. This view shows No. 150109 departing northwards. The signal box was abolished in 2012. On the left is the branch to Stourbridge Town. Said to be the shortest branch line in Europe, the shuttle service on the line is currently operated by a pair of Class 139 Parry People Movers.

The view north at Kingswinford. The lines straight on lead to the Round Oak steel terminal. In the centre background is the Brierley Hill terminal. The line which curves behind the signal box is the Pensnett branch. This line originally extended to Oxley and had one of the longest gestations of any line; the first section was completed in 1858 but it was to be another sixty-seven years before it was opened throughout, and just seven years after that it lost its passenger service. All that remains today is the 2 miles to Pensnett.

No. 60015 heads away south with a train of steel coil. The OWW line now ends just north of here where it meets the South Staffordshire line at Dudley. The section between there and Wolverhampton has long been closed and lifted. Kingswinford signal box was burnt down in 2001.

Wolverhampton Low Level, the terminus of the OWW, seen on 21 July 1990. Following its closure to passenger trains in 1972, the station became a parcels depot until 1981. The main station building has listed status; the rest has been demolished and redeveloped for various commercial uses.

The South Staffordshire Railway

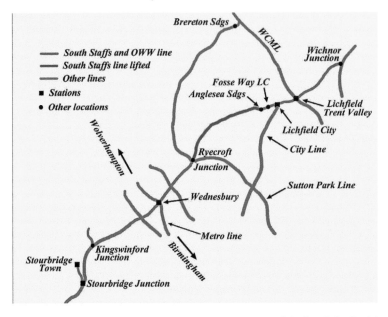

The South Staffordshire Railway was formed from the amalgamation of the South Staffordshire Junction and the Trent Valley, Midlands and Grand Junction Railways. The SSR was leased by the LNW in 1861 and absorbed by it in 1867. The line lost its passenger service in 1964 and the section from Ryecroft Junction to Anglesea Sidings closed to all traffic in March 1984. The line continued in use for freight until 1993. A number of plans have been put forward over the years, and the current plan is for the line to be reopened between Wednesbury and Brierley Hill as an extension of the Midland Metro, and also for freight.

Shortly before closure of the line, No. 37713 heads past Wednesbury Town signal box with a Bescot–Round Oak trip working on 11 March 1993. The signal box was destroyed by arsonists in 1995.

Nos 37077 and 37040 pass through Wednesbury with train 6V69 bound for Cardiff Tidal Sidings. The abutments to either side of the train are the remains of the bridge that once carried the Birmingham, Wolverhampton & Dudley Railway across the SSR tracks. Opened in 1854 as a broad gauge line, it was converted to standard gauge ten years later. The line closed in 1972 except for a branch at Handsworth connecting to Smethwick Junction, and the section from Wednesbury to Bilston, which was retained to service a scrapyard. In 1995 the 4 miles between Snow Hill and Smethwick were reopened as part of the Jewellery Line. Four years after this, the line was reused for the Midland Metro.

No. 31530 *Sister Dora* is seen with an engineer's train in the Exchange Sidings at Wednesbury. This area is now the location of the Metro Centre depot and control room. No. 31530 went through a number of identities, starting out as D5695, then becoming successively Nos 31265 and 31430 and finally its present number. It has been preserved at Mangapps Railway museum. 11 March 1993.

Ryecroft Junction was the meeting point of the Sutton Park line and the lines to Rugeley and Lichfield. No. 31537 is arriving from the Sutton Park line with an engineer's train. The Class 31/5s were 31/4 locomotives that had had their ETH gear removed on transfer to the CE department. 18 April 1995.

Between Lichfield and Anglesea Sidings the SSR remains open as a freight branch. Here we see No. 60068 *Charles Darwin* approaching Fosse Way level crossing with the Brownhills Depot–Lindsey fuel oil empties. 20 July 1995.

Lichfield is the northern terminus of the Cross City Line, which runs from Lichfield to Redditch. Each pair of home signals controlled access from the Up loop or the Up platform line to the Sutton Coldfield or the Anglesea Sidings line. The Up and Down loops, the signals and signal box have all gone, and the line is now electrified. 25 March 1990.

A Class 150 leaves the station with the diverted 14.13 Birmingham to Lincoln. The trackwork here has been considerably reduced. 25 March 1990.

This train, having arrived in the Down platform at Lichfield Trent Valley, has proceeded to the crossover beyond the signal box in order to switch to the Up line. It is seen as it runs back towards the station. This procedure is no longer necessary as the station now only has one platform in use, which is signalled bi-directionally. 3 July 1991.

Although the Wolverhampton & Walsall Railway received its Act in 1865, it took another eight years to build this short stretch of line. The LNW bought the W&W but then sold it to the Midland, who were building a line from Castle Bromwich to meet it. This line opened in 1879. The original W&W closed in 1964 and the remaining section between Walsall and Castle Bromwich lost its passenger service the following year. It remains open for freight. Nos 20165 and 20128 approach Rushall Canal Bridge with a short freight on 20 July 1995.

The SSR built a branch from Walsall to Cannock in 1859 in order to exploit the Cannock Chase coalfield, while the Cannock Mineral Railway built the line from Cannock to Rugeley; both were later absorbed by the LNW. The line lost its passenger service in 1965 but this was progressively restored between 1989 and 1998. Electrification of the line is due for completion in 2017. On 22 July 1994 No. 60073 *Cairn Gorm* approaches Brereton Sidings signal box with 6T58, the Rugeley Power Station to Essington Wood Opencast. This is now the site of Rugeley Town station.

Birmingham Area

The line from Whitacre to Birmingham Lawley Street was opened by the Birmingham & Derby Junction Railway in 1842. The 09.00 Cardiff–Nottingham in the shape of a Class 158 passes Washwood Heath Sidings No. 1 signal box. The box has since been abolished. 30 June 1993.

No. 60004 *Lochnagar* heads westbound at Washwood Heath with a loaded MGR. The Class 60 was one of the last types of diesel locomotives supplied to British Railways. A total of 100 machines intended for heavy freight duties were supplied between 1989 and 1993. The locomotives are equipped with the Mirrlees Blackstone eight-cylinder, 145-litre 8MB275T engine, giving 3,100 hp. 30 June 1993.

At Bromford Bridge No. 47845 passes the British Steel sidings with the 11.06 York to Swansea on 30 June 1993. There was once a station at Bromford Bridge, which was open only on race days. It closed in 1965.

The railway to the Austin Rover plant at Longbridge was the last vestige of the Halesowen Railway, a joint venture of the GWR and MR, built in 1883. A station was provided at the works during the First World War, when the factory was being used for munitions production. Public passenger services ceased in 1919, although workmen's trains continued until 1960. On 26 February 1995 shunter *Emma* is seen with car transporter wagons. Everything in this view no longer exists – the tracks, signal box, even the works themselves, have all been obliterated.

Tyseley South Junction is the meeting point of the ex-GWR lines from Stratford-upon-Avon and Leamington Spa. The 14.23 Shirley to Birmingham Snow Hill hurries past.

Further north is Caledonia Yard. A Class 117 unit resplendent in chocolate and cream livery passes the yard with the 15.35 Snow Hill to Dorridge. Caledonia Yard is currently out of use. 30 June 1993.

North Staffordshire

In 1995, No. 56123 *Drax Power Station* passes Etruria station with a train for the BSC Shelton works. The station was named after the nearby Wedgwood ceramics factory, the name of which derives from Etruria in Italy, an area famed in ancient times for its pottery. Etruria station was opened by the North Staffordshire Railway in 1848 and closed in 2005. BSC Shelton is also closed, as is the Etruria factory.

Nos 37407 and 37429 top and tail the Branch Line Society's railtour at Winkhill on the Caldon Low branch. The branch was built by the North Staffs to connect the NSR system at Leekbrook with the Leek & Manifold Light Railway at Waterhouses. It opened in 1905, the year after the Leek & Manifold. That railway closed in 1934 and the Caldon Low branch lost its passenger service in 1960; however, it stayed open for freight traffic until 1989, principally to service the quarries at Caldon Low. It has now been purchased and incorporated into the Churnet Valley Railway preservation operation. 16 April 1994.

At Silverdale Colliery, No. 60057 runs round its train. In later years the colliery had a production of 1 million tons per annum. It closed in 1998. The buildings and platform are of Silverdale station. With the Newcastle to Market Drayton line, the North Staffs Railway reached its furthest point west, and it was opened in stages between 1850 and 1870. West of Silverdale passenger services ceased in 1956, and between Silverdale and Stoke in 1964. Madeley to Market Drayton was closed to all traffic in 1966.

Now with its loaded train, No. 60057 arrives at Madeley Road station. A chord was opened here in 1962 connecting the Market Drayton line with the WCML. The loco will run round here before hauling its train on to the WCML Down slow line. Madeley station was opened in 1870, then renamed Madeley Manor to avoid confusion with the LNW station on the main line. It later became Madeley Road and was closed to passengers in 1931, apparently generating a saving for the LMS of some £92 per annum! Following closure of Silverdale Colliery, the connection with the WCML was severed. 24 May 1992.

Oxford to Cambridge

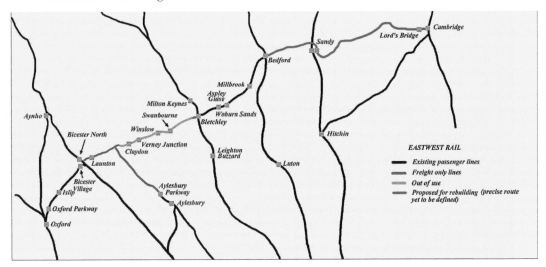

The Oxford–Cambridge line was opened in stages. The Bedford Railway was created in 1845 with the aim of building a railway from Bedford to Bletchley. Built by that company, the line was opened in November 1846 and was worked from the outset by the London & Birmingham Railway, which, as the LNWR, absorbed the Bedford Railway in 1879. The Buckingham Railway was responsible for building the railway from Bletchley to Banbury, which opened in May 1850. The line from Verney Junction to Oxford followed a year later. The earliest part of the Bedford–Cambridge line to be built was the 4-mile-long Sandy & Potton Railway, which opened in June 1857. The Bedford & Cambridge Railway took over this company and completed the line throughout in in 1862. It, in its turn, became part of the LNWR.

Little changed for the next hundred years until, as part of the 1955 Modernisation Plan, a flyover was built at Bletchley to avoid trains on the east–west axis having to thread their way across the station layout. It was intended that the Oxford–Cambridge line would be developed as a transversal axis, particularly for freight. However, in 1959 the line was proposed for total closure. This did not happen and neither was the line included in the 1963 Beeching cuts. Nevertheless in 1968 Bedford–Cambridge closed completely; Bletchley–Oxford lost its passenger service, while Bletchley–Bedford survived, due in part to the substantial traffic emanating from the Stewartby brickworks. Lord's Bridge is the first station after Cambridge on the Cambridge–Bedford line. It is currently used by the university as the site for an observatory.

The 17.50 Bletchley–Bedford arrives at Lidlington. The cream hut seen behind the cyclist is for the crossing keeper, who controlled the signals from a ground frame. Lidlington is now the site of the Marston Vale Signalling Control Centre, which controls operation of the whole line. 3 July 1991.

Aspley Guise, and No. 31456 approaches the station with a train of waste material destined for Forder's siding. Note the manual operation of the crossing gates, now replaced by full barriers, remotely controlled by CCTV. 31 May 1989.

Also on 31 May, a Class 108 DMU arrives at Woburn Sands with a Bletchley–Bedford service. The signal box has since been abolished. Like the other stations on the line built by the Bedford Railway, the station buildings have a pleasant *cottage orné* style.

In April 1990, when this photograph was taken, the station at Winslow was still in relatively good order. Since then the buildings have been demolished and the site has become overgrown. It has long been realised that this line should never have closed and there are plans now in hand for at least a partial reopening. This project – East West Rail – has begun with the completion of the route through to Oxford from Bicester, and the construction of a new chord at Bicester to allow the introduction of Marylebone–Oxford services, from December 2016. Completion of Oxford–Bletchley was originally scheduled for 2017, but this was later put back to 2019. Currently there is no firm date. In December 2016 the Secretary of State announced that the line would be the subject of a 'vertically integrated' contract in the hope that this would speed up the reopening of the line. For the reopening a new Winslow station will be built on a different site.

Swanbourne is the only station between Oxford and Bletchley to have retained its original buildings. Seen here on 9 April 1990, the buildings are still in the original maroon and cream of the London Midland Region. In 1947 Swanbourne had a service of nine trains a day to Bletchley. For the reopening of the line, apart from the rebuilding of the line and the construction of new stations, there are other problems. The chord connecting Bletchley with the Oxford line has long been removed. As a result, the platforms for Bletchley will have to be built alongside the flyover. Services calling at Milton Keynes will not be able to continue to Bedford without a reversal at Bletchley. Since this is not planned to happen, there will be alternating services of Oxford to Bedford and Oxford to Milton Keynes. Milton Keynes–Aylesbury services are also planned. The likelihood of the rebuilding of the line between Bedford and Cambridge would seem to be very small indeed.

Verney Junction, named after Sir Harry Verney of Claydon House, was once the meeting place of the lines from Banbury and Quainton Road, as well as the Oxford–Cambridge line; something hard to believe from this view taken in 1990. This was not the only station to be named after Sir Harry. It was only in order to inherit his cousin's estates in 1827 that Sir Harry changed his name to Verney; it had previously been Calvert, the name used for the station just south of Claydon L&NE Junction, on the GCR line.

Claydon station in 1975, with its station buildings still relatively complete. Nothing now remains.

Hertfordshire Railtours' 'The Mothball', headed by No. 56046, passes through the remains of Launton station. This was the last passenger train to traverse the line. 29 May 1993.

Oxford and Banbury

The GWR opened its broad gauge line to Oxford on 12 June 1844. The Oxford & Rugby Railway started to build its line the following year; it was taken over by the GWR and the line to Banbury was completed by 1852. The line reverted to standard gauge in 1872. Oxford has always been an important calling point on cross-country routes. On 4 May 1981, the 07.21 Liverpool to Poole is in the hands of No. 45113 as it pulls away from the station.

At Banbury in 1990, the Liverpool–Poole service is hauled by a Class 47. The last of the Class 45s were withdrawn two years earlier. The train waiting to leave is the 09.30 Brighton to Edinburgh. In 1974 Banbury was transferred to the London Midland Region but the GWR heritage is quite clear. The semaphore signals disappeared when the station was resignalled in 2016, with both Banbury North and Banbury South signal boxes being abolished. 18 March 1990.

Between Banbury and Oxford is King's Sutton. In the BR Blue era a Class 47 heads south with a rake of Mk 1 coaches. The tiny King's Sutton station can be seen in the background. 17 August 1980.

Cheltenham & Great Western Union Railway

At Kemble station a Class 156 DMU leaves with the 10.46 Cheltenham to Swindon on 11 July 1990. On the right is the platform for the former branch to Cirencester, which closed in 1965. Cirencester was the terminus of the line from Swindon between 1841 and 1845, at which time the line from Kemble to Cheltenham was completed. At Kemble there was also a branch to Tetbury, which closed at the same time as the Cirencester branch.

The Great Central Joint Lines

At the time this photograph was taken on 30 May 1989, Great Missenden signal box, dating from 1892, was the last remaining Metropolitan Type 1 box still in use. It was abolished the following year but remained in place for a further twenty years until it was moved to the Mid-Hants Railway. A Class 115 unit approaches with a Marylebone–Aylesbury service.

In order to reach London, the MSL, shortly to become the Great Central, obtained running powers on the Metropolitan's Verney Junction–Aylesbury–London line as far as Harrow, from where it built its own independent line to Marylebone. The Metropolitan/Great Central Joint Committee was set up in 1906. A Class 115 DMU arrives at Aylesbury with a service from Marylebone. Preparatory work for the resignalling of the whole line is already evident. Network SouthEast had been in existence since 1986 but not all vehicles have been repainted. These Class 115 units were particularly associated with services out of Marylebone; they were replaced by the new Class 165 units in 1991/2. 30 May 1989.

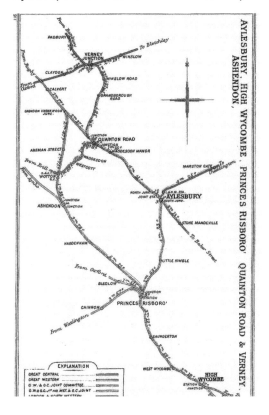

Congestion on the Metropolitan line led the Great Central to seek another route to London. At the same time the GWR was looking for a way to shorten its route to Birmingham. The two companies decided to build a new line from High Wycombe to Northolt Junction, from where each company would have their own independent line into London. The GCR built a connection from Grendon Underwood to Ashendon Junction and the GWR built its line north to Aynho to join up with the line from Didcot. This work was completed by 1910. The GWR/GCR Joint Committee controlled the lines from Ashendon Junction to Northolt Junction and Princes Risborough to Aylesbury. The section of railway between High Wycombe and Princes Risborough was part of the GWR route from London to Aylesbury via Maidenhead, and opened in 1863.

An Aylesbury–Marylebone service arrives at Princes Risborough. This was once a four-way junction, with lines to Watlington, Oxford via Thame, Aynho and Aylesbury, hence the need for the large signal box seen in the background. Princes Risborough North, built in 1904 and with a 126-lever frame, is the largest surviving GW box. It was abolished in 1991, when the line was re-signalled. Grade II listed, it has been restored and is now open to members of the public. 29 May 1989.

Part of the Oxford branch survived to access the oil terminal at Thame but this remaining section closed in 1991. Some years earlier, 'Skinheads' Nos 31138 and 31185 come off the Thame branch with a train of tanks bound for Ripple Lane, on 23 April 1980.

At High Wycombe a Class 115 unit stands at Platform 3 with a service for Marylebone. Everything in this view has changed: the through lines have been removed, the semaphore signals have gone, and of course the Class 115 units no longer ply this route. 29 May 1989.

At Beaconsfield the through lines are still in place but are in the process of being removed, no longer being necessary.

Wales

Borders

The line from Wrexham to Chester came into being as part of the North Wales Mineral Railway and was opened in November 1846. There were stations at Saltney, Rossett, Gresford and Wrexham. These were joined by Balderton in 1901 and later by the halt of Rhosrobin. Decline set in in the 1960s and all the intermediate stations were closed. In 1995 No. 56018 is seen with an Elgin–Dee Marsh service at Gresford.

Following absorption by the GWR, the line became part of the GWR main line between Paddington and Birkenhead. It would be tempting to think that at one time in steam days GWR 4-6-0 No. 6024 *King Edward I* worked up Gresford Bank, but in fact the Kings only worked as far as Wolverhampton or Shrewsbury. This is 21 September 1991 and No. 6024 is hauling the Welsh Marches Express.

The Shrewsbury & Chester Railway was formed from the merger of the North Wales Mineral Railway and the Shrewsbury, Oswestry & Chester Junction Railway. It opened throughout in October 1848 and became part of the GWR in 1854. Whittington station was closed in 1960; the signal box was abolished in 1992 and the crossing converted to automatic half barriers. The box is a McKenzie & Holland Type 3 dating from 1881.

The Oswestry branch lost its passenger service in 1966 but was retained for freight. At the time this photograph was taken in May 1991 the line had been out of use for several years. This view shows Oswestry South signal box and the main station building, which was the headquarters of the Cambrian Railway. A preservation group hopes to be running trains into Oswestry before too long.

Just south of Wrexham is Croes Newydd. This photograph was taken in 1962 and shows the view looking south. Pannier tank No. 1660 is in the Up goods loop. (Photograph Ben Brooksbank)

At the same location on 18 May 1991, No. 37138 heads south with an empty steel train. The Up goods loop and the Watery Road sidings, on the right, are still there. Coming in from the left is the goods branch from Minera.

Four years later, the sidings have disappeared under a housing development. The goods loop is still there and No. 56018 is in the process of running round its train before heading back north along the Wrexham, Mold & Connah's Quay line to Dee Marsh. This is the train seen earlier on Gresford Bank.

The Wrexham, Mold & Connah's Quay Railway opened its line from Wrexham to Buckley in 1866, which was extended to Shotton and Hawarden Bridge in 1889. The WM&CQ became part of the GCR in 1905. Remarkably, there are no less than nine stations on this 14-mile stretch of line. In June 1995 unit No. 153367 arrives at Hawarden Bridge with the 11.33 Wrexham–Bidston.

Central Wales

The first section of the Cambrian main line to be completed was the Llanidloes & Newton Railway, which opened in 1859. Oswestry to Weshpool followed in 1860 and the Newton & Machynlleth Railway in 1863. The junction between the L&N and the N&M was at Moat Lane, a short distance to the east of Caersws station, seen here on 16 June 1991. A track machine waits to enter the single line section to Newtown. Caersws signal box is a Dutton Type 1, constructed for the Cambrian Railways in 1891. It retains its Dutton 18-lever frame. It is no longer active, the line now being controlled from Machynlleth.

Machynlleth is the next station west of Caersws, some 22 miles further on. The intervening five stations were all closed in June 1965. On 16 June 1991, a Class 150 stands in the Down platform, next to Machynlleth's *cottage orné* station buildings, with the 14.35 to Aberystwyth. The line was extended to Aberystwyth in 1864.

Seen from the castle, a pair of Class 150s cross at Harlech station on 22 October 1986. The signal box has now closed and the line is controlled from Machynlleth. (Photograph Chris Gwilliam)

North Wales

The Chester & Holyhead Railway was conceived essentially to connect Britain and Ireland. The 59¾ miles from Chester to Bangor opened in May 1848, with a service of four trains each way daily. From the outset the railway was worked by the LNW and was taken over by it in 1859. On 25 May 1990, No. 71000 *Duke of Gloucester* crosses the River Dee just west of Chester with the North Wales Coast Express. The first bridge across the Dee was designed by Robert Stephenson and completed in 1846. In 1847 it failed disastrously under a train, causing the deaths of five people. The one-time quadruple nature of the tracks is clear from this photograph.

On 2 May 1992, a Class 156 heads past the former Mold Junction depot with the 15.01 Crewe to Holyhead. The depot closed in 1966. Mold Junction signal box, seen in the background, was abolished in 2005 together with the Up goods line, seen in the foreground.

With an excursion for Llandudno on 16 August 1989, one of Tyseley's Class 115 units slows for the signal at Sandycroft. Note the quadruple track here. The West Midlands Passenger Executive logo seen on the rear coach was only used until 1990; since that time, the signal box has been abolished and the Up and Down slow lines have been lifted. Sandycroft station, of which no trace remains, was opened in 1884 and closed in 1961.

More evidence of the former quadrupling is seen at Shotton Low Level, where new platforms had to be erected when the station was reopened in 1972, having only closed six years earlier. No. 37422 heads through with a Birmingham–Holyhead service. In the background is the bridge that carries the platforms of Shotton High Level.

On 20 April 1981, a pair of Class 103 DMUs approach Flint station with the 12.20 Bangor–Manchester Victoria. Considered non-standard, all of these Park Royal units were withdrawn by 1983. Three vehicles have survived into preservation.

At Holywell on 24 June 1993, No. 37509 heads east with an engineer's train. The appearance of quadruple track is given by the Up and Down goods loops, which at this time were over a mile long. Holywell Junction signal box will be abolished when the North Wales signalling is completed in early 2018.

Point of Ayr Colliery, in full production in 1992. Four years later mining ceased, and now nothing remains here.

Classes 156 and 158 form the 14.01 Crewe–Holyhead. Talacre signal box is on the left and Point of Ayr Colliery in the background. Talacre station opened in 1903 and closed in 1966, and Talacre signal box is also now closed. 2 May 1992.

On an overcast August day in 1989, No. 156403 heads eastbound away from Rhyl, passing under Rhyl No. 1 home signal gantry.

On the same day, No. 47611 arrives with a Euston–Holyhead service. Since this photograph was taken, the Up fast and Up bay lines have been removed. The signals and signal box at Rhyl are due to be abolished by early 2018. No. 1 box, visible here, is an LNW Type 4 dating from 1900 and is a listed building.

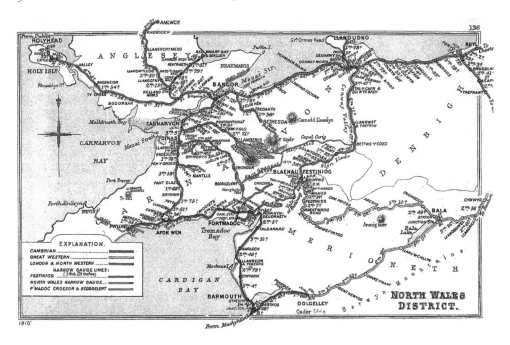

The railways of north-west Wales as they were in 1914.

On 23 August 1989, Bulleid Pacific No. 35028 *Clan Line* restarts the North Wales Coast Express away from Llandudno Junction. The station became a junction in 1858 with the opening of the 3-mile-long branch to Llandudno, followed in 1863 by the branch to Blaenau Ffestiniog. The present station dates from 1897.

This is the Glan Conwy freight depot at Llandudno Junction. From left to right: coal depot; engineer's siding; oil depot. Nothing whatsoever remains of this depot. The whole area has been redeveloped.

On 23 August 1989, a Derby Lightweight three-car unit arrives at Llandudno, passing the LNW Type 4 signal box dating from 1891. The signal box survives, as does the gantry, but the bracket signals have gone.

The branch to Llandudno station was opened in 1863, and the present station dates from 1897. This image of Llandudno station was taken in August 1989, with a selection of old and new DMUs on view. This scene has changed dramatically; Platforms 4 and 5 on the left-hand side have gone completely and been replaced by a car park, while the station roof has been re-glazed.

The Ynys Mon Express, headed by No. 71000 *Duke of Gloucester*, approaches the closed station of Gaerwen Junction on 25 May 1992.

No. 47458 *County of Cambridgeshire* pulls away from Gaerwen signal box with 09.05 Euston–Holyhead. The train had stopped there for 20 minutes, apparently in some kind of trouble.

Gaerwen station opened in 1849 and became a junction in 1864 when the Anglesey Central Railway opened its line to Llangefni, extending to Amlwch in 1867. In 1908 a branch from Holland Arms to Red Wharf bay was added. This branch closed in 1950 and the Amlwch line closed to passengers in 1964, but remained open to serve the Octel factory near Amlwch. This traffic ceased in 1993. Before that, in 1992, a series of shuttles were run between Gaerwen and Amlwch using a Derby Lightweight unit, which is seen here near Llangefni. Discussions about reopening have taken place since then but without any concrete result.

AMLWCH BRANCH (WEEK DAYS ONLY.)‡

	a.m.	a.m.	p.m.	B (Thurs days only.)	p.m.	p.m.	p.m.	
Amlwch ...dep	7 30	11 10	2 0	...	5 25	7 39	...	
Rhosgoch	7 38	11 19	2 9		5 34	7 48	...	
Llanerchymedd...	7 47	11 30	2 20		5 45	7 59	...	
Llangwyllog	8 0	11 39	2 29		5 54	8 8	...	
Llangefni	8 7	11 50	2 39	4 50	6 5	8 18	...	
Holland Arms	8 17	11 56	2 46	4 56	6 11	8 24	...	
Gaerwen ...arr	8 26	12 5	2 55	5 3	6 20	8 34	...	
Bangor ...arr	8 48	1 3	3 15	5 25	7 7	8 53	.	
Holyhead ,,	10 10	1 0	3 45	5 48		9 51	...	

	a.m.	a.m.	B noon	noon	p.m.	p.m.	p.m.	
Holyhead dep	...	7 45	...12 0	3 15	6 0	8 5	...	
Bangor...... ,,	4 25	9 10	12 15 12 I 5	4 5	4 50	8 53	.	
Gaerwen ...dep	4 50	9 35	12 58	12 55	4 25	6 45	9 15	...
Holland Arms ...		9 42	12 45	1 2	4 32	6 55	9 22	.
Llangefni	5 6	9 50	12 50	1 10	4 40	7 3	9 30	.
Llangwyllog	.	9 59		1 20	4 49	.	9 39	.
Llanerchymedd...	5 37	10 8		1 28	4 58	...	9 48	.
Rhosgoch	5 49	10 18		1 38	5 7	.	9 57	.
Amlwch ...arr	6 0	10 29		1 49	5 18	...	10 8	...

‡—Mondays excepted.

B—Trains marked **B** run through to and from Bangor.

I—Leaves at 12.15 **noon** on Thursdays.

The timetable for 1896.

No. 31421 has replaced the failing No. 47458 for the return Holyhead–Euston working and is seen passing through Ty Croes station, running considerably late, on 25 May 1992.

The present station at Holyhead, seen here, dates from 1866. Although the original station opened in 1848, through services from Chester had to wait until the completion of Stephenson's bridge across the Menai Strait. The first through train ran from Holyhead to Euston on 18 March 1850. This photograph, taken on 17 June 1993, shows a Class 37 waiting to leave with a service for Birmingham. The container depot on the right has since been demolished and the area turned into a car park. (Photo Ben Brooksbank)

South Wales

The Newport, Abergavenny & Hereford Railway opened to goods in July 1852 and to passengers in January 1854. The NA&H did not actually reach Newport but met the Monmouthshire Railway & Canal Company's line at Pontypool, which it used to reach Newport. Of the original nine stations between Hereford and Pontypool, only Abergavenny remains open. In this view, a pair of Class 155 units depart with the 13.42 Crewe to Cardiff on 15 July 1990. Note that the lower quadrant up starter has below it an upper quadrant calling-on signal.

No. 37301 heads west past Llanwern West Junction on the Down relief line with a short engineer's train. One of the great success stories of the dieselisation programme was this Type 3 locomotive, the Class 37. Equipped with the English Electric 12CSVT engine delivering 1,750 hp, the Class 37 proved itself to be a popular and reliable machine. Introduced in 1960, a total of 309 were built and a number remain in service today with various private operators. (Photograph Chris Gwilliam)

In April 1981, a Class 126 InterCity set is seen approaching Maindee East Junction with a Gloucester–Cardiff working. These three-car units spent most of their working lives in Scotland; all were withdrawn by 1983. Four vehicles have survived into preservation and are to be found at the Bo'ness & Kinneil Railway. (Photograph Chris Gwilliam)

On the same day, No. 33025 passes with a Portsmouth–Cardiff train. No. 33025 has survived into preservation and is now owned by West Coast Railways. (Photograph Chris Gwilliam)

In June 1995, No. 60034 is seen on the Down relief line with an empty ore train. In the background on the Down main is No. 60062 with an empty steel train. The lines on the left lead to Ebbw Vale.

The line to Ebbw Vale was built by the Monmouthshire Railway & Canal Company. It lost its passenger service in 1962 but the line was kept open by the passage of trains servicing the steelworks at Ebbw Vale. The steelworks closed in 2002 but happily a passenger service was reinstated in 2008, with stations at Rogerstone, Risca, Crosskeys, Newbridge, Llanhilleth and Ebbw Vale. In 1993 No. 60033 is seen hauling a rake of steel coil through Crosskeys on the surviving section of double track, which stretches from Crosskeys Junction to Risca South Junction.

In October 1985, No. 45020 approaches Cardiff Central with a Llandarcy–Llanwern oil train. Cardiff Central station came into being when the South Wales Railway opened its line from Chepstow to Swansea in 1850. The original station was replaced by a new station in the early 1930s. The Class 45s were nearing the end of their days when this photograph was taken, with No. 45020 lasting only until the end of the year. (Photograph Chris Gwilliam)

Class 116 set C375 arrives at Radyr with the 13.58 Cardiff–Merthyr Tydfil on 26 March 1989. This scene has changed dramatically; beyond the junction to the right were the extensive sidings of Radyr Yard and the Radyr Reclamation Depot, but neither any longer exists. The junction has also been considerably modified and the number of signals reduced. The line straight on leads to Cardiff via Queen Street, and the line to the right to Cardiff via Ninian Park. A new signal box has been constructed and is situated on the opposite side of the tracks to the old one, which can just be seen behind the right-hand group of signals. Note the mechanical route indicator and the fixed distants. Set C375 did not last very much longer, being scrapped the following year.

The next station north of Radyr is Taff's Well. Somewhat oddly, the signal box at the station was known as Walnut Tree Junction. This junction, which was situated just in front of the Class 150 unit heading away from the station, was with the Rhymney Railway line from Aber Junction, Caerphilly. The signal box, which is a listed structure, has been abolished and moved elsewhere. 20 February 1992.

North of Taff's Well the line divides at Pontypridd for Treherbert, and again at Abercynon for Hirwaun and Merthyr Tydfil. The line to Merthyr was the original Taff Vale main line, built incidentally with the advice of Brunel, and, opening in 1841, was the first main line steam railway in Wales. No. 150281 passes Black Lion Junction with a Merthyr–Penarth service. Black Lion signal box has been abolished and the track layout here simplified.

Bargoed is a station in the Rhymney Valley opened by the Rhymney Railway in 1858. The Rhymney's original route to Cardiff was via Taff's Well, but this was replaced by a direct route in 1864. Unit No. 150232 calls with the 12.53 to Barry Island. Bargoed retains its signal box, but the line has been singled beyond the station.

The line to Barry Island was opened by the Barry Railway Company in 1896, essentially for people making day trips to the seaside and funfair. The scene in this photograph, taken on 22 February 1992, has changed completely: the signal box and signals have gone; the line on the left has been retained for national rail services; the centre line has been lifted; and the line on the right is now used by the Barry Tourist Railway, part of the Barry Railway Centre. There is also now a fence along the centre of the platform on the right.

On 28 February 1992, No. 37703 passes through Aberthaw Yard with a rake of empty HAA wagons from Aberthaw Power Station. Class 37/7 locomotives were specially adapted for heavy freight haulage. This scene has changed considerably: the 1897 Barry Railway Type 2 signal box remains but much of the trackwork has been removed and Class 37s no longer haul HAA wagons to the power station. Interestingly, the number 37703 was chosen both by Lima and Vitrains for their Class 37/7 model. The Vale of Glamorgan line lost its passenger service in 1964 as part of the Beeching cuts, but was kept open by trains for Aberthaw Power Station and Ford's at Bridgend. It was also used as a diversionary route. Passenger services were reinstated in 2005 with new stations at Llantit Major and Rhoose. The line was scheduled to be electrified under the Great Western electrification scheme, but this has now been deferred indefinitely.

Tondu was once an important junction. The line in the foreground is the freight-only line from Margam, and the line to the left is the Llynfi Valley line to Maesteg. The line to the right leads to Bridgend; opened in 1861, this was originally a broad gauge line. The line in the distance curving away to the right once led to a whole group of lines, branching out from Brynmeyn Junction. The only survivor of this group is the line to Blaengarw, which is currently being developed as the Garw Valley Railway heritage line. At the time this photograph was taken in February 1992 there were no passenger services at Tondu – the last, to Maesteg, having been withdrawn in 1970 – but in September 1992 a service was reinstated between Bridgend and Maesteg. This scene has changed completely: the old footbridge has been replaced and a new platform built for the restored passenger trains. Tondu signal box still stands, although operating far fewer signals.

Thirty years earlier, Tondu was considerably busier. 2-8-0T No. 4243 heads though the station with a trainload of coal slack from Ogmore Valley. 1 June 1962. (Photograph Ben Brooksbank)

West Wales

These photographs, taken at Swansea Docks in June 1993, provide an excellent illustration of the decline of rail freight in recent years. No. 08756 takes a train of coal into the King's Dock.

The shunter now moves wagons from Marcroft Engineering back to Burrows Yard.

Marcroft Engineering shunter *Gillian* rearranges some Sea Urchin wagons. *Gillian* was built by Thomas Hill in 1967 for the National Coal Board; she arrived at Marcroft in 1993 but left the following year and was scrapped in 1996. Marcroft Engineering closed this facility in 2003.

No. 08756 returns from Ford's Elba works with more wagons destined for Burrows Yard. The Ford factory is now closed.

A general view of Burrows Yard. There is now no rail activity at the yard, at King's Dock or in fact anywhere shown in the foregoing photographs.

No. 08756 is seen once again, this time shunting at Briton Ferry Yard on 1 June 1993.

Pantyffynnon is near the southern end of the 88-mile-long, single-track Heart of Wales line, which stretches from Craven Arms to Llandeilo Junction. In this view, the driver of single unit No. 153318, forming the 13.05 Swansea to Shrewsbury, accepts the token from the signalman at Pantyffynnon signal box for the section as far as Llandeilo. Today the line is controlled using the radio-controlled token block system. The line on the left leads to the Gwaun-Cae-Gurwen branch. 19 February 1992.

No. 08993 passes the former station of Pontyates with a rake of HEA wagons bound for the Cwm Mawr disposal point. This locomotive was one of a class of five, designated 08/9, with specially cut-down cabs to work the line to Cwm Mawr. This was necessitated by the low bridges on the line, which had started life as a canal. The Burry Port & Gwendreath Valley Railway started freight operations in 1869, with passenger services following in 1909, but the latter lasted only until 1953. The last freight train ran on 29 March 1996. 19 February 1992.

A Class 116 unit, wearing Valley Trains branding, arrives at Ferryside with a westbound service. These units, introduced in 1957, were originally all allocated to the Western Region but were later to be found elsewhere on the network. The last were withdrawn in 1995. Ferryside signal box is considered to be the best surviving example of a Great Western Type 3 box and is a listed building.

Class 108 No. S958 approaches Ferryside station with the 11.16 Pembroke Dock to Swansea train on 20 February 1992.

Carmarthen became connected to the rail network in 1852 with the arrival of the broad gauge South Wales Railway. Since the closure of the line to Aberystwyth, Carmarthen has been a terminal station. In torrential rain Standard 4MT 2-6-4T No. 80079 leaves with the Carmarthen–Swansea leg of the Pembroke Coast Express on 30 May 1993.

A railway to Fishguard was planned as early as the mid-nineteenth century; however, changing minds and abandoned plans meant that the railway did not reach the harbour of Fishguard until 1906. On 30 May 1993, LMS 4-6-0 No. 44767 *George Stephenson* is seen at Manorowen on the 1 in 50 climb away from Fishguard with the Pembroke Coast Express.

The South West

Bristol Area

Bristol Temple Meads station. Bristol was reached from London in 1840. Brunel's original station proved inadequate by the 1870s and a new station was built. The arched train shed is in the background; to the left of this are the parcels platforms and to the right are the platforms added in 1935. On the extreme right are the lines leading to Bristol Bath Road Depot. An HST leaves with a train for the South West on 8 April 1995.

On 8 April 1995, a Motorail van sits at Bristol Temple Meads, waiting for its customers. Services from Bristol were available to St Austell, Newcastle and Stirling. All Motorail services ceased a few weeks after this photograph was taken.

The Bristol & Exeter Railway headquarters at Bristol. The building was designed by Samuel Fripp and was completed in 1852. It is a listed building. The B&E had its own station at Bristol, constructed of wood; it was popularly known as the 'Cowshed'.

Bristol Bath Road Depot was built on the site where the 'Cowshed' once stood. It was converted to a diesel depot in 1960, and is seen here just a few weeks before closure in May 1995.

In 1995 No. 60034 *Carned Llewelyn* heads towards Westerleigh oil terminal with a train of tanks. Westerleigh branch is the surviving stub of the Midland route to Bristol and Bath. Passenger trains on this route ceased in 1966, while freight lingered on until 1971.

Hallen Marsh Junction. The line through Avonmouth to Severn Beach was the result of the efforts of three different companies: the GWR, the Midland, and the Bristol Port Railway & Pier Company. The passenger service to Severn Beach has been threatened with closure several times but has managed to survive and has a two-hourly service for most of the day. In this view we see No. 155368 heading towards Bristol. The line curving to the left in the background is to Severn Beach; those curving to the right lead to Filton junction, and those in the right foreground formerly led to a number of industrial establishments.

No. 47316 heads north through Hallen Marsh Junction with a train of car transporters. The Class 47 was built by Brush Traction. It was equipped with the Sulzer 12LDA28-C engine, which was an up-rated version of the engine fitted to Classes 45 and 46. This uprating was a mistake; the twelve-cylinder Sulzer had already been uprated from 2,300 hp in the Class 44 to 2,500 in Classes 45 and 46, and this further uprating to 2,750 was a step too far. The engine started to suffer stress fractures and to cure this problem the engine was down-rated to give 2,580 hp, little more than in the earlier classes. A total of 512 machines were produced, a number of which remain in service.

West of England Main Line

The Bristol & Exeter opened its broad gauge line as far as Bridgwater in 1841. Yatton was the second stop west of Bristol; the station buildings are to designs by Brunel. The station was originally named Clevedon but was renamed Yatton when the B&E opened a branch to Clevedon in 1847 and a branch along the Cheddar Valley to Wells and Witham followed in 1869; both branches closed in the 1960s. The bay for Clevedon was where the cars are now parked. Leaving a rather tatty looking station on 8 April 1995 is an HST bound for Bristol. Despite its appearance, Yatton is a listed station.

In the early 1930s the tracks were quadrupled between Taunton and Norton Fitzwarren, and Taunton station was completely rebuilt. The need for this measure is apparent when it is realised that at the time Taunton was at the convergence of lines from Bristol, Minehead, Barnstaple, Exeter, Chard, Yeovil and Castle Cary. Today only the mile-long section through Taunton station remains as quadruple track. Taunton was reached by the B&E in July 1842. The locomotive for the inaugural run from Paddington to Exeter on 1 May 1844 was the 2-2-2 *Orion* of the Firefly class, designed by Daniel Gooch and on this occasion driven by him. The train left Paddington at 07.31 and arrived at Exeter at 12.45. An HST heads away from the station on the Up main.

Fairwater Yard is to the west of Taunton; it currently deals with ballast cleaning trains. An HST heads towards Exeter. The High Speed Train, also known as the InterCity 125, was introduced in 1975/76 and transformed services on the Great Northern and Great Western main lines. The power cars were originally equipped with the Paxman Valenta engine (12RP200L) running at 1,500 rpm and developing 2,250 hp, but all have now been re-engined with either the Paxman VP185 or the MTU 16V4000R41R.

Cullompton station was opened in 1844, the same year that the tracks reached Exeter. Cullompton, along with a number of other locations, saw tracks quadrupled through the station in the early 1930s. This accounts for the distance between track and platforms evident in this view. The quadrupling was removed in the 1960s and the station closed in 1964. On 24 April 1992 the 15.35 Paddington to Penzance passes through. The goods shed, seen on the right, has long been demolished and the site redeveloped.

Wilts, Somerset & Weymouth Railway

On 14 July 1990 a Derby Lightweight unit waits to leave Westbury with the 12.15 Southampton to Bristol. Westbury first appeared on the railway map when the Wilts, Somerset & Weymouth Railway opened its line from Thingley Junction on 5 September 1848.

There was little activity by the WS&W for the next two years, except that in March 1850 the company was absorbed by the GWR. In October that year a branch to Frome was completed, and another from Frome to Radstock started, although that line was not completed until 1854. Frome station, seen here in 1990, is the last surviving GWR station with an overall roof and is listed Grade ll.

Yeovil Area

The WS&W finally reached Yeovil in September 1856, and Weymouth the following January. The station in Yeovil was Pen Mill. Unit No. 150273 arrives with the 09.00 Weymouth to Bristol.

The Salisbury & Yeovil Railway was completed in June 1860, meeting the LSWR line from Exeter at Yeovil Junction. On 25 April 1992, the 09.15 Waterloo to Exeter arrives behind No. 47708. Yeovil Junction signal box, seen in the background, was abolished in 2012; the area is now controlled from Basingstoke.

Arriving from the opposite direction on the same day is No. 47716 *Duke of Edinburgh's Award* with the 10.25 Exeter–Waterloo. Both Nos 47708 and 47716 were in a small sub-class previously based in Scotland, fitted with equipment enabling them to operate in push-pull mode.

There was a third station at Yeovil, Yeovil Town, which, opened in 1860, was joint between the B&E, the GWR and the LSWR. The B&E had in fact reached Hendsford, a little to the west, with their line from Durston as early as 1853. The Durston–Yeovil line closed in 1965 and the Town station a year later. Clifton Maybank was a goods-only station, originally provided for transfer between the broad gauge GWR and the standard gauge LSWR.

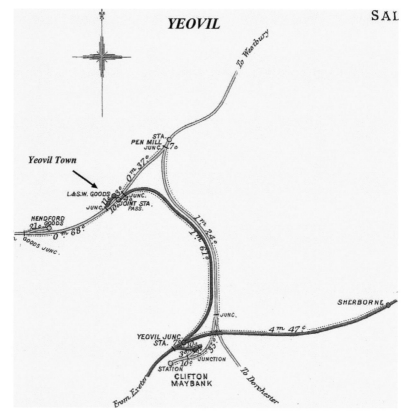

Sherborne, just to the west of Yeovil, was reached by the railway in May 1860. Today Sherborne enjoys an hourly service to Waterloo or Exeter provided by Class 158 or 159 units.

Exmouth Junction

A view of Exmouth Junction taken from above Blackboy Tunnel. The coal concentration depot is on the left. These depots were set up in the 1960s to replace what had previously been the case, with each station receiving its own supplies. A Class 108 unit heads for Exeter. The line to the right is to Exmouth and beyond the coal depot is the plant maintenance depot. Everything to the left seen here is now covered with a forest of silver birch trees and fenced off. The coal depot ceased operations not long after these photographs were taken on 24 April 1992.

A view taken in the other direction. The train is the 14.21 Barnstaple–Exmouth. Where the coal depot had been set up was previously the site of the Southern Railway concrete works. The Southern Railway and then BR produced a large range of concrete products, including bridges, lamp posts, goods sheds and platelayers' cabins.

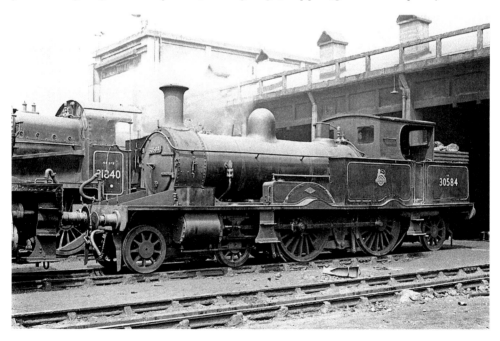

The new engine shed at Exmouth Junction which was constructed in the 1920s was also built of concrete. It closed in the mid-1960s and was demolished. On 6 June 1960, Adams Class 415 4-4-2 No. 30584 sits outside the shed. It was withdrawn the following year. (Photograph Peter Groom)

The Dorset Coast

At Wareham a Class 442 Wessex Electric unit stands with the 14.32 Waterloo–Weymouth. These 100 mph units were introduced in 1988 to coincide with the extension of electrification from Bournemouth to Weymouth. The railway reached Wareham in 1847 with the opening of the Southampton and Dorchester Railway, sometimes referred to as 'Castleman's Corkscrew' on account of its somewhat circuitous route. Castleman was chairman of the company.

The line from Worgret Junction to Swanage closed to passengers in 1972. The line remained open to the LPG/oil sidings at Furzebrook, seen in this photograph in April 1992. A preservation group was set up to create a tourist line on part of the Swanage branch and in 2002 its line was reconnected to the national network. From 2017 a summer passenger service started operating between Swanage and Wareham for two years on an experimental basis. The first train ran on 13 June and was top and tailed by Nos 33012 and 37518.

Prior to electrification the Bournemouth–Weymouth line was worked by Class 33s operating in push-pull mode with 4TC sets, as seen here. In August 1987 No. 33155 blasts away from Wool with a Weymouth–Waterloo service. Note that the electric third rail is already in place. The Class 33 was equipped with a Sulzer 8LDA28 engine, giving 1,550 hp. A total of ninety-eight were built, originally exclusively for the Southern Region, but later years saw them used extensively elsewhere. An incredible total of twenty-nine have survived into preservation. (Photograph Chris Gwilliam)

Castleman's Corkscrew took an inland route through Dorset via Ringwood and Wimborne, thus avoiding the coastal town of Bournemouth. This was not thought to be a problem as, at that time, Bournemouth was little more than a hamlet. Bournemouth was finally reached by railway in 1870 when the LSWR opened a branch from Ringwood. Four years later the Poole & Bournemouth Railway approached the town from the opposite direction, completing its line to Bournemouth West on 15 June 1874. Branksome was on this stretch of line but the station itself did not open until 1893. On 23 April 1992, No. 37803 heads through the station with a steel train.

At Branksome Junction 4-Vep unit No. 3529 heads towards Bournemouth. The lines to the right formerly led to Bournemouth West, which closed in 1965, and now lead to the Bournemouth Traction Depot. 23 April 1992.

Bournemouth Central opened in July 1885. Despite its rather tatty appearance it is in fact a listed station. In April 1992 a 'Wessex Electric' waits to leave for London. When Castleman's Corkscrew bypassed it in 1847, Bournemouth consisted of just thirty houses. Today, together with the adjoining towns of Poole and Christchurch, it has a population of 465,000.

South Devon

The South Devon Railway was designed by Brunel as an atmospheric railway and by January 1848 passengers were being carried as far as Newton Abbot by atmospheric trains. Pipes were laid as far as Totnes, but they were never used, as by September 1848 Brunel had to acknowledge that the experiment was a failure and the railway reverted to conventional operation as a broad gauge line. Between Teignmouth and Dawlish, a Down HST emerges from Parson's Tunnel in April 1986. (Photograph Chris Gwilliam).

Above left: On the same day, No. 47482 heads east with a rake of Mk 1 coaches. This section of line was not doubled until 1884, by which time the South Devon had been absorbed into the GWR. Along with all other GWR lines it became standard gauge in 1892. (Photograph Chris Gwilliam)

Above right: The South Devon had a number of branches, most of which are now closed. In 1866 a line was opened to Moretonhampstead. This closed to passengers in 1959 but the line as far as Heathfield has remained open for freight. This view taken near Heathfield shows the English China Clay works, apparently disused at this time. Since this photograph was taken on 24 April 1992, the line has occasionally been used by freight trains, including for timber traffic. Track remains in place and there are moves to reopen the line for both passenger and freight.

Below: At one time it was possible to travel beyond Barnstaple in one of four different directions. Today the only possibility is to travel southwards to Exeter. In a depleted looking station, a Class 101 DMU waits to depart with the 13.01 to Exeter on 26 October 1990.

The route of the LSWR to Plymouth was by way of Okehampton and Tavistock. The station looks remarkably complete on 25 October 1990, eighteen years after closure. The line remained in place to service the quarry at Meldon, 3 miles beyond the station. Okehampton has experienced something of a revival in recent years: Great Western Railway runs trains between Exeter and Okehampton on summer Sundays and the Dartmoor Railway Association runs a shuttle service between the station and Meldon Viaduct on Saturdays, Sundays and bank holidays, also in the summer.

The station before Okehampton is Sampford Courtenay, which features as one of the UK's least used stations; in 2014/15, 196 passengers used the station. The station sees a service of four return trains on summer Sundays provided by Great Western Railway.

The 165-metre-long Meldon Viaduct was completed in 1874, having been started in 1871. After the line was closed to passenger traffic the bridge was used as a shunting neck by trains accessing Meldon Quarry. In 1990 it was deemed too weak for further rail use and the track was lifted. It is one of only two surviving wrought iron viaducts in England and is a scheduled monument.

Cornwall

The route surveyed by Brunel for the Cornwall Railway received its Act in 1846 but it was to be another thirteen years before the broad gauge line between Plymouth and Truro was completed. At Liskeard on 25 October 1990, No. 47811 waits to leave with the 12.40 Penzance to Paddington.

An HST arrives at Liskeard with the 10.35 Paddington–Penzance. In 1876 the fastest journey from London to Penzance took exactly twelve hours; in 1949 it took just under seven hours, and today takes just over five hours. Note the subsidiary signal, which controls access to the Looe Valley line.

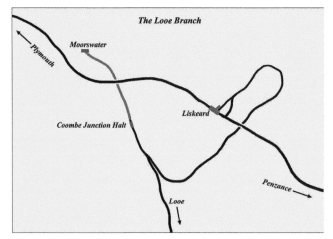

The Looe branch owes its existence to the Looe & Caradon Railway, which opened a line from Moorswater to Caradon in 1844. The Liskeard & Looe Railway extended the line from Moorswater to Looe in 1860. Until 1901 there was no connection to the GWR station at Liskeard; in that year a line from Coombe junction to Liskeard was completed, terminating in a platform at right angles to the main line platforms.

Class 121 'Bubble Car' No. 55026 stands at the Looe platform waiting to depart with the 14.06 to Looe. Of the sixteen original members of this class, no less than ten have been preserved. Sadly, No. 55026 is not one of them. 25 October 1990.

The railway from Fowey to Newquay originally had no connection to the main line at Par. This was not built until 1892, when the broad gauge main line was converted to standard gauge. The line has always been important for china clay traffic and on 26 October 1990 No. 37669 heads away from St Blazey towards Burngullow Junction with a train of CDA china clay hoppers.

Goonbarrow Junction is the only crossing place along the 20-mile section between St Blazey and Newquay. A pair of Class 121 units pass through the junction with the 09.47 Newquay to Par train on 26 October 1990.

On 26 October 1990, No. 47801 arrives with the 12.40 Penzance to Paddington at Truro. The broad gauge West Cornwall Railway opened from Penzance to Truro in 1855. It was converted to a mixed line in 1866/7.

At Truro, the driver of the Class 101 unit preparing to depart for Falmouth returns to his train with the train staff for the branch. The staff also has a key to unlock the ground frame at Falmouth, giving access to the harbour branch. October 1994. (Photograph Chris Gwilliam)

A Penzance–Paddington HST arrives at St Erth on a very wet October day in 1990.

St Erth is the junction for the St Ives branch. Class 122 'Bubble Car' No. 55012 arrives at St Erth with the 14.52 St Ives–Penzance on 26 October 1990. Built by the Gloucester Carriage & Wagon Works in 1958, No. 55012 is now preserved at the Weardale Railway.